AnimalWays

Tigers

AnimalWays

TIGERS

Rebecca Stefoff

Benchmark Books

MARSHALL CAVENDISH
NEW YORK

With thanks to Dr. Dan Wharton, director of the
Central Park Wildlife Center, Wildlife Conservation Society,
for his expert reading of this manuscript.

Benchmark Books
Marshall Cavendish
99 White Plains Road
Tarrytown, NY 10591-9001
Website: www.marshallcavendish.com

Text copyright © 2003 by Rebecca Stefoff
Map copyright © 2003 by Marshall Cavendish Corporation
Map by Carol Matsuyama
Illustrations copyright © 2003 by Ka Botzis

Library of Congress Cataloging-in-Publication Data
Stefoff, Rebecca, 1951–
Tigers / by Rebecca Stefoff.
p. cm. — (Animalways)
Summary: Presents detailed information on tigers, including their representation in art
and mythology, physical evolution, various subspecies, habitats, physical characteristics,
behavior, life cycle, and interaction with humans, as well as the efforts being made to pro-
tect remaining subspecies from extinction.
Includes bibliographical references (p. 101) and index (p. 102).
ISBN 0-7614-1391-X
1. Tigers—Juvenile literature. [1. Tigers. 2. Endangered species.] I. Title. II. Series.
QL737.C23 S724   2002   599.756—dc21   2002000079

Photo Research by Candlepants Incorporated

Cover Photo: Corbis / Keren Su

The photographs in this book are used by permission and through the courtesy of:
Corbis: Tom Brakefield, 2, 36, 78–79; Keren Su, 9, 12, 57, 93; Kennan Ward, 14; Janez
Skok, 19; Gallo Images, 21, 66; Tiziana and Gianni Baldizzone, 22; W. Perry Conway, 33,
42, 77; Stuart Westmorland, 34; William Dow, 49, 71; Frank Lane Picture Agency, 50, 69,
73; Reuters NewMedia, 59; David A. Northcott, 61; Joe McDonald, 75; Chase Swift, 87;
James Marshall, 90; AFP, 91; Jim Zuckerman, back cover; *Art Resource, NY*: Giraudon, 11;
Photo Researchers: Tom McHugh, 25; Field Museum, 27; Renee Lynn, 38; S.R. Maglione,
41; Alan & Sandy Carey, 83; Nancy Sefton, 89; Terry Whittaker, 96; *Animals Animals*:
A. & M. Shah, 53; Gerard Lacz, 65; *Getty Creative*: Stone/Renee Lynn, 54–55.

Printed in Italy

6 5 4 3 2 1

Contents

Animal Kingdom

CNIDARIANS

coral

ARTHROPODS
(animals with
jointed limbs and
external skeleton)

MOLLUSKS

squid

CRUSTACEANS

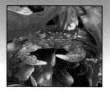

crab

ARACHNIDS

spider

INSECTS

grasshopper

MYRIAPODS

centipede

CARNIVORES

TIGER

SEA MAMMALS

whale

PRIMATES

orangutan

HERBIVORES
(5 orders)

elephant

				PHYLA

ANNELIDS

earthworm

CHORDATES
(animals with
a dorsal
nerve chord)

ECHINODERMS

starfish

**SUB
PHYLA**

VERTEBRATES
(animals with a
backbone)

CLASSES

FISH

fish

BIRDS

gull

MAMMALS

AMPHIBIANS

frog

REPTILES

snake

ORDERS

RODENTS

squirrel

INSECTIVORES

mole

MARSUPIALS

koala

SMALL MAMMALS
(several orders)

bat

1

"Lord of Land Animals"

At the beginning of the twentieth century, a European traveler named Perceval Yelts visited the remote and mountainous province of Yunnan in southwestern China to study the customs and arts of the people there. He later described their beliefs about two mighty animals, one mythological and the other real. "Just as the dragon is chief of all aquatic creatures," Yelts wrote in 1912, "so is the tiger lord of land animals. . . . The tiger symbolizes military prowess. It is an object of special terror to demons and is therefore painted on walls to scare malignant spirits away from the neighbourhood of houses and temples."

Sleek, strong, and swift, the tiger claims an important place in the myths and folklore of many Asian cultures. Tigers once roamed across much of Earth's largest continent, from the shores of the Caspian Sea in the west to Siberia in the northeast and the tropical island of Bali in the southeast. During the twentieth century, however, the tiger's range shrank dramatically. Today, the

A TIGER IN NORTHERN CHINA, WHERE PEOPLE ONCE VIEWED THE MARKINGS ON THE ANIMAL'S FOREHEAD AS THE SYMBOL THAT MEANS "KING" IN CHINESE SCRIPT. FOR THOUSANDS OF YEARS, THE TIGER HAS BEEN HONORED IN A VARIETY OF WAYS BY THE CULTURES OF CHINA AND OTHER ASIAN COUNTRIES.

world's biggest cats live in just a few parts of eastern and southern Asia. But as symbols of power and ferocity, of protection and good fortune, and of the living force of nature, tigers have left their mark in images and stories over a much wider region.

Myths and Lore

The Amur River flows through the pine forests of northeastern Asia, with Siberia on the north and China on the south. In the 1930s, archaeologists working on the banks of the Amur discovered a group of 150 boulders on which the prehistoric inhabitants of the region had carved symbols such as horned elk, snakes, and masked faces. One boulder bore the image of a striped cat: the Siberian tiger. Scientists estimate that the boulder was carved between 4000 and 3500 B.C., making it one of the oldest known tiger images.

The tiger remained important to the people of Siberia well into modern times. Anthropologists who visited the tribes north of the Amur River early in the twentieth century reported that some groups regarded the *amba*, or tiger, as a sacred animal, the ruler and protector of the forest. They never hunted tigers, even when the great cats carried off their dogs, and anyone who killed a tiger was driven out of the tribe.

China has been home to several subspecies, or varieties, of tiger. The great striped cats appear in many Chinese myths, artwork, and traditional customs. Some stories say that long ago the founder of Taoism, a body of ancient Chinese magical and religious beliefs, discovered the secret of eternal life and rose to heaven on the back of a tiger. The image of a tiger was believed to keep bad luck and evil spirits away. Parents placed tiger-shaped silver charms on newborn sons to bring them good fortune, and mothers embroidered tiger eyes on their children's shoes to guide them through life. Nightmares were said to be prevented by sleeping on tiger-skin pillows, travelers draped their horses and luggage with tiger skins for protection from the hazards of the road, and people decorated their homes with painted tigers on scrolls and screens to prevent demons from entering. In the Chinese calendar, each year is identified with one of twelve animals. The tiger is one of these animals, and people born in a Year of the Tiger were thought to have power over evil spirits. The people of Tibet, southwest of China, also had magical beliefs about the tiger. They covered the thrones of high-ranking priests and rulers with tiger skins, which were

A CHINESE ARTIST CARVED THIS TIGER IN WHITE JADE DURING THE HAN DYNASTY, WHICH RULED CHINA FROM 206 B.C. UNTIL A.D. 220.

A traditional Chinese toy in the form of a tiger. Parents believed that the tiger's image harnessed the animal's strength to provide protection and good fortune for their children.

thought to give protection from snakes and harmful insects. In both China and Tibet, when tiger skins or claws were not available, people turned to the written word, trying to treat illnesses such as fevers by reading poems about tigers.

Most tigers in art are golden-brown striped with black, as are most tigers in life. But on rare occasions, black-striped white tigers are born, identical to other tigers except for a difference in pigment, which affects their coloring. Traditional cultures regarded these white tigers as creatures of exceptional power and value. The white tigers known today are a mutation belonging to the tiger subspecies that is native to India, and they are bred in captivity. Some researchers, however, think that at least a few wild white tigers may have existed in China in earlier eras, for the white tiger came to occupy a special place in Chinese mythology as a symbol of the god of the west and of autumn. The white tiger brought wind and rain—storms that could be destructive but were also life-giving, to an agricultural civilization that depended on rainfall. Pai Hu, as the white tiger god was called, was immortal and could live in the heavens, either in the moon or in the stream of stars called the Milky Way.

People in Korea, China's neighbor, also respected tigers, especially white tigers. They believed that the two guardians of their country were the Blue Dragon and the White Tiger, and they regarded the tiger as the messenger and companion of San Shin, the beloved god of the mountains. Koreans greatly valued tiger skins, which they believed had magical protective qualities. In former times, brides carried tiger skins in their wedding processions in the hope that the skins would bring happy marriages and many children. Tigers are now almost extinct in Korea, but pieces of striped cloth still appear at some weddings, filling the symbolic role of the skins.

Tigers were once numerous in the jungle-covered mountains of Southeast Asia. In the traditional lore of the Hmong people, who live in the highlands of Vietnam, Laos, and Cambodia, the tiger is the king of all animals and a supernatural being. One Hmong story illustrates the tiger's power and wisdom. A tiger was ready to eat a cow, until the cow begged the tiger to spare her so that she could feed her young calf. The calf then begged the tiger to eat it instead of its mother. The tiger was so impressed with the love of the cow and calf for each other that

it spared both of them. The Hmong called the tiger "lord of the forest" or "king of the mountain," and they believed that tigers killed only sinful people. Anyone slain by a tiger, therefore, must have committed a sin that deserved that fatal punishment. At any spot where a tiger had killed a person, the Hmong set up memorial stones—to the tiger. Such a memorial would include a small altar where people could make offerings to the spirits of the tiger and the forest. The respect the Hmong felt for the tiger was so great that if a tiger fell into one of the pit traps they built to catch deer, they roped it, pulled it out, and set it free, with their apologies. If tigers troubled a village, the people would move their village rather than hunt the tigers. One British observer suggested a practical origin for Hmong tiger worship: The people had come to regard tigers as sacred protectors because the tigers killed the deer and wild pigs that raided their rice fields and destroyed their crops.

Tigers also ruled the forests farther south, in the Southeast Asian regions that are now the nations of Malaysia and Indonesia. The word for *tiger* was sometimes considered too sacred to utter—the Malay people traditionally referred to the animal as "the striped prince" or "old hairy face." Some groups had shamans, healers who were believed to have magical or super-natural powers that allowed them to connect the human and spiritual worlds. Often these shamans claimed to have a special link with tigers, and they acted as though they were possessed

---

WHITE TIGERS BELONG TO THE SAME SPECIES AS OTHER TIGERS. THEY ARE NOT ALBINO ANIMALS; RATHER, A MINOR GENETIC MUTATION PRODUCES THEIR WHITE FUR AND BLUE EYES.

---

by tiger spirits. Mircea Eliade, one of the founders of modern anthropology, described a session in which a *pawang*, or a Malay shaman, asked his tiger spirit to cure a sick man: "The *pawang* did in effect turn himself into a tiger; he ran on all fours, roared and licked the patient's body for a long time as a tigress licks her cubs."

On the island of Sumatra, now part of Indonesia, certain regions were thought to be the haunts of were-tigers, people who could turn themselves into tigers by night. Whole communities called tiger villages were said to be inhabited by were-tigers. Such beings were believed to be harmless to humans when in their tiger form. When in their human form, they looked just like everyone else, except that their upper lips were smooth, without the groove found on the lips of true humans. Sometimes, however, their behavior revealed their identity, as in the tale of a man who, while visiting a village, became ill and vomited up chicken feathers. The villagers then knew that he was the were-tiger who had eaten their chickens the previous night. They did him no harm, because both tigers and were-tigers were sacred beings. The murder of a tiger might bring about some terrible natural disaster, such as a flood or a volcanic eruption. Another aspect of Sumatran tiger lore concerns *silat minang-kabau*, the island's traditional martial art. The movements of this fighting art are said to be based on the movements of a tiger, and the most skilled teachers of the art are rumored to be the tigers' kin.

The notion of kinship between humans and tigers occurs in many parts of the animals' former range. A legend of the Naga people of northeastern India says that the first man and the first tiger were brothers, born to the same mother. The man stayed home and the tiger went to live in the forest. One day they met and fought. The tiger was stronger, but the man managed to kill it with trickery and poison. From the body of the dead brother came forth hundreds of tigers to populate the hills and plains of India.

Tigers stalk through the myths and tales of many of India's cultures. The Warlis, a people who traditionally lived north of the Indian city of Mumbai (Bombay), worshipped a tiger god named Vaghadeva, whose statue stood on the edge of every village. People sang and danced before the statue, which represented life and fertility. Special priests of the tiger god practiced herbal healing, and Vaghadeva presided over marriage ceremonies in the form of striped shawls worn by the bride and groom. In another part of India, the Gond people left offerings of meat at shrines dedicated to Waghai Devi, the tiger goddess.

India is a land of many religions, and the tiger has a place in most of them. Buddhism, which originated in northern India, has a legend about a prince who went out walking and came upon a tigress with two cubs. Thin and starving, the desperate tigress was about to devour her own cubs, but the generous-hearted prince threw himself down before her so that she could eat him instead. The tigress was too weak with hunger to attack him, so he drew his own blood with a thorn. She licked the blood and grew strong enough to consume all but his bones. The kind prince was later discovered to have been the Buddha himself in one of his earthly lives, and Buddhists built a shrine upon the spot where his noble sacrifice was said to have taken place. The religion of Islam entered northern India long ago, and Muslims there occasionally made scroll paintings that showed holy men riding tigers, symbols of the strength with which they attacked evil in the world. But the most widespread image of the tiger in India is related to the Hindu myth of the powerful goddess Durga, who brings light to the world. She is usually portrayed astride a tiger, which she rides into battle against darkness and demons. The tiger, Durga's guide and a vital part of her strength, represents the energy of the earth and of nature. Pictures of Durga riding a tiger often decorate shops, homes, and the sides of trucks and buses.

People and Tigers

People and tigers have lived together in Asia for thousands of years. Some traditional societies did not hunt tigers, but others did. A tiger might be slain because it threatened a community or had killed humans. Many more tigers were killed for their skins, teeth, or other parts of their bodies that were considered valuable or were used in rituals or traditional medicines. Live tigers were tokens of great wealth, and although capturing tigers isn't easy, people sometimes did so on the orders of their rulers. In late-nineteenth-century China, for example, various provinces made yearly payments to the emperor in the form of tiger skins and live tigers. Hunters baited traps with pigs to catch the tigers.

These killings and captures may have reduced tiger populations in some areas, but they did not seriously threaten the survival of the species. Beginning in the eighteenth century, however, the European presence in Asia increased. More areas came under the control of Britain, France, and other European powers, and more European explorers and hunters began venturing into remote and wild regions where tigers abounded. They profoundly changed the balance of humans and tigers that had existed for so long. The Europeans had guns, and some of them, especially the British, came from cultures that hunted for sport. They regarded wild animals as trophies to be shot. Although many Europeans admired tigers, they did not consider the animals as sacred, supernatural, or symbolic of nature's majesty. Instead, tigers were impressive game for hunting, and

A Hindu *sadhu*, or holy man, displays a tent ornamented with the image of a tiger during the Khumb Mela religious festival in Allahabad, India. In Hindu mythology, the tiger is related to the powers that fight darkness and evil.

the source of valuable skins. Often they were seen as dangerous nuisances that had to be eliminated to protect human life in villages, towns, and farms. For example, forests chosen to provide wood for new projects such as railway lines and bridges were cleared of tigers that might attack laborers and thereby interfere with progress.

The Europeans killed tigers at a greatly increased rate, and their example led some Asians to do the same. The era of British rule in India—especially the nineteenth century and the first part of the twentieth—was a bad time for tigers. British soldiers and sportsmen, as well as local rulers, killed the great cats on a grand scale. In *The Tiger's Destiny* (1992), Valmik Thapar, a native of India and an authority on tiger conservation, writes, "Over the last few centuries, killing a tiger has been seen as a symbol of manhood for some of those who ruled India, and countless important people have roamed the forests trying to prove themselves. I have been through records which show that at least 20,000 tigers were shot between 1860 and 1960." One legendary British hunter "bagged" 100 tigers in the Rajasthan district of India in 4 years. Another claimed a lifetime total of more than 300. But European hunters were outdone by Indian maharajahs, or princes, who organized elaborate hunts for themselves and their honored guests. Armed men on foot or riding elephants would beat their way through large tracts of forest, driving all game animals, including tigers, into a small area where they could easily be shot. At one such hunt, held in the Himalayan kingdom of Nepal on India's northern border in 1911, King George V of England and his friends shot 39 tigers. Some Indian princes killed astonishing numbers of tigers over many years of hunting. In 1965, for example, the maharajah of Surguja, then an old man, told wildlife biologist George Schaller that his tiger kills numbered "one thousand and fifty only."

DATING FROM 1814, THIS ILLUSTRATION OF A TIGER HUNT REFLECTS THE SPORTING
SPIRIT THAT LED TO THE SLAUGHTER OF THOUSANDS OF TIGERS.

Over the centuries, people have reacted to the tiger in ways
ranging from worship to slaughter. By the end of the twentieth
century, the deadly combination of hunting and habitat loss had
made the tiger one of the most endangered of the large mammal

Decked with tiger skins, the living room of the palace of the Maharajah of Dungapur, India, is a memorial to the era when tiger hunting on a grand scale was a favorite pastime of European sportsmen and Indian princes alike.

species in the world. Humans now control the tiger's fate. Their choices will determine whether it survives or becomes extinct. But in a world without guns, a world in which the human population was not growing at an explosive rate, tigers would be supreme predators. They evolved over millions of years to fit that role.

2 Tigers Yesterday and Today

Many species of ancestral felines, the forerunners of modern cats, existed in earlier ages. They became extinct and vanished long ago, but they left fossil remains—massive, powerful skeletons and teeth like swords—that awe modern museumgoers. They also left their descendants, the thirty-seven species of cats known today, including *Panthera tigris*, better known as the tiger.

Feline Origins

A clue to the earliest known feline ancestors lies in the diet of today's cats. All cats are carnivores, or eaters of meat. Paleontologists think that all kinds of carnivores, including cats, descended from very ancient meat-eating mammals called miacids. The miacids were small and probably resembled weasels. Their chief foods were most likely insects and worms. Yet they were

AMONG THE TIGER'S EXTINCT RELATIVES WERE SEVERAL KINDS OF SABER-TOOTHED CATS, INCLUDING SPECIES BIGGER THAN THE LARGEST TIGERS THAT EXIST TODAY.

hunters—they are the oldest known animals equipped with car-nassial teeth, the strong rear teeth with which carnivores tear meat—and they probably preyed on other small mammals. The miacids flourished around 65 million years ago. The world's biggest carnivores, the dinosaurs, had recently become extinct, and their disappearance allowed the miacids to take over the role they had filled. The miacids evolved into two broad groups of carnivores.

Scientists call one of these groups the Aeluroidea, or aeluroids, from a Latin word meaning "catlike." The other group consisted of the bearlike Arctoidea, or arctoids. Over millions of years, each group became more diverse. Species died out, and others appeared to take their place. By about 40 million years ago, the aeluroids had evolved into several families. Among these were the Hyaenidae (hyenas) and the Felidae (cats). This is why cats and hyenas are more closely related to each other than either is to dogs, which evolved from the arctoid line. A third aeluroid family, the Nimravidae, contained many catlike animals. Scientists sometimes refer to the Nimravidae as pale-ofelids, or ancient cats. All nimravids or paleofelids had become extinct by 2 million years ago, leaving no descendants in the modern world. The family of Felidae, also called the neofelids or true cats, gave rise to all of the cat species that exist today as well as to many species that have become extinct.

Paleontologists are still working to sort out the complex evo-lutionary histories of both the paleofelids and the neofelids. One thing they do know is that both families included species of large carnivores with long, curved teeth at the front corners of their upper jaws. These extinct species are sometimes grouped together under the name "sabertoothed cats" because their immense teeth reminded early fossil hunters of sabers, or curved swords. "Sabertoothed tiger" is also used occasionally,

IN THIS ARTIST'S DRAWING, A *SMILODON* CONFRONTS AN IMMENSE EXTINCT BIRD CALLED A *TERATORNIS*.

but none of the prehistoric sabertoothed cats was a tiger. And not all of the extinct sabertoothed animals were cats—species with similar teeth evolved in at least two families in addition to the paleofelid and neofelid cat families.

Fossil finds suggest that most of the paleofelid species were sabertoothed. The best known of the extinct sabertoothed cats, however, is a species called *Smilodon fatalis* that belonged to the neofelid or true cat family. *Smilodon* appeared around 2 million years ago and became extinct quite recently, in geological terms—only 10,000 years ago or so. Numerous fossils of this mighty beast have been found in North America. About 2,000 specimens of *Smilodon* come from a single place, the La Brea Tar Pits in Los Angeles, California. Scientists believe that the great cats ventured into the sticky pools of naturally occurring tar to feed on animals that had been trapped there. The predators also became trapped and died in the tar, which preserved their remains.

Neither *Smilodon* nor any other sabertoothed cat was a direct ancestor of today's cats. Instead, all living cat species (and some extinct ones) descended from an ancestral neofelid that lived around 12 million years ago. This species evolved into various lines of descent leading to modern cats. The first of these lines to appear was the ocelot line, followed by the ancestors of cheetahs, pumas, and various small cats. Some time after 3 million years ago, another line of neofelids evolved into the ancestors of lions, tigers, leopards, and jaguars. The oldest fossil tigers date from approximately 2 million years ago and were found in southeastern China. Paleontologists think that this region was the birthplace of the tiger.

Modern Tiger Subspecies and Their Ranges

Scientists use a system of classification called taxonomy to organize living things into groups on the basis of shared characteristics. Scientific classification begins with very large groups called kingdoms (such as the plant kingdom or the animal kingdom) and proceeds through a series of categories, each more narrowly defined than the last, to the species level. According to this system, the tiger belongs to the kingdom Animalia, the phylum Chordata, the subphylum Vertebrata (animals with backbones), the class Mammalia (all mammals), the order Carnivora (all carnivores), the family Felidae (all cats), the genus *Panthera* (which includes five kinds of big cats), and the species *tigris*.

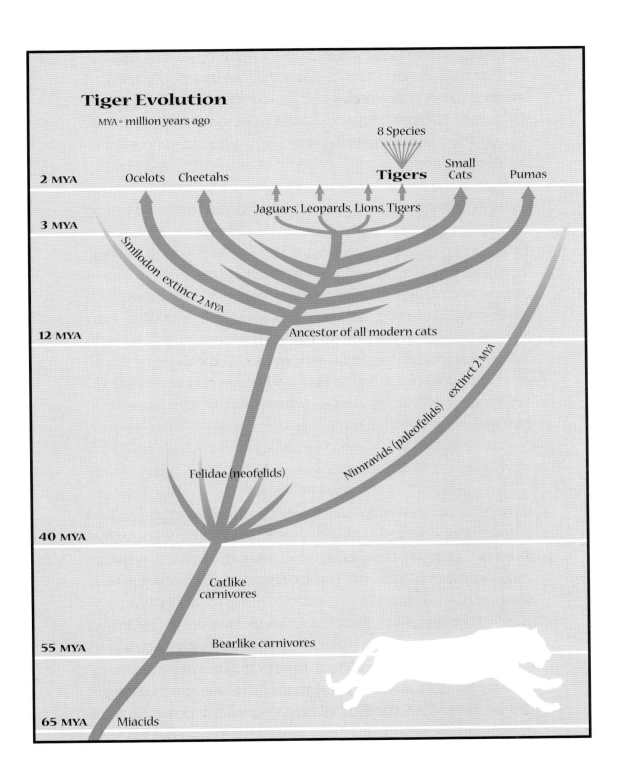

Tiger Evolution

MYA = million years ago

8 Species

2 MYA — Ocelots · Cheetahs · **Tigers** · Small Cats · Pumas

Jaguars, Leopards, Lions, Tigers

3 MYA

Smilodon extinct 2 MYA

12 MYA — Ancestor of all modern cats

Nimravids (paleofelids) extinct 2 MYA

Felidae (neofelids)

40 MYA

Catlike carnivores

55 MYA — Bearlike carnivores

65 MYA — Miacids

Tigers are the largest living cats, averaging 9 to 10 feet (2.7 to 3 m) from nose to tail tip—about 32 inches (80 cm) of that length is tail. A tiger's average height at the shoulder is around 42 inches (105 cm). A typical adult tiger weighs between 300 and 600 pounds (135 and 270 kg), and males are generally bigger than females. Lengths and weights significantly greater than average have been recorded for some individual wild tigers (captive tigers do not set size standards or records because animals raised in captivity are often larger than those in the wild). Tigers are usually yellow, golden brown, or orange-red in color, fading to white or cream on the belly, around the eyes and mouth, and on the insides of the legs. They are striped with black, dark gray, or brown in a pattern that is as unique to each tiger as fingerprints are to humans. Wildlife scientists use stripe patterns to identify the tigers they study.

All tigers belong to the species *Panthera tigris* (sometimes abbreviated to *P. tigris*), but scientists have divided the species into smaller groups called subspecies based on differences in physical features and home territory. A hundred years ago there were eight tiger subspecies, but only five exist today. Three became extinct during the twentieth century. Each of the eight subspecies has—or had—its own name, geographic range, and characteristics. Scientists studying tiger genetics have found that the differences between subspecies are very small. The populations have not been separated long enough for major genetic changes to take place.

Panthera tigris amoyensis, known as the South China tiger or Amoy tiger, is probably the oldest subspecies. According to paleontologists, certain features make its skull more primitive than the skulls of other tiger subspecies. Its brain case is smaller, and its eye sockets point more directly forward. Scientists think that these features link the South China tiger most directly with

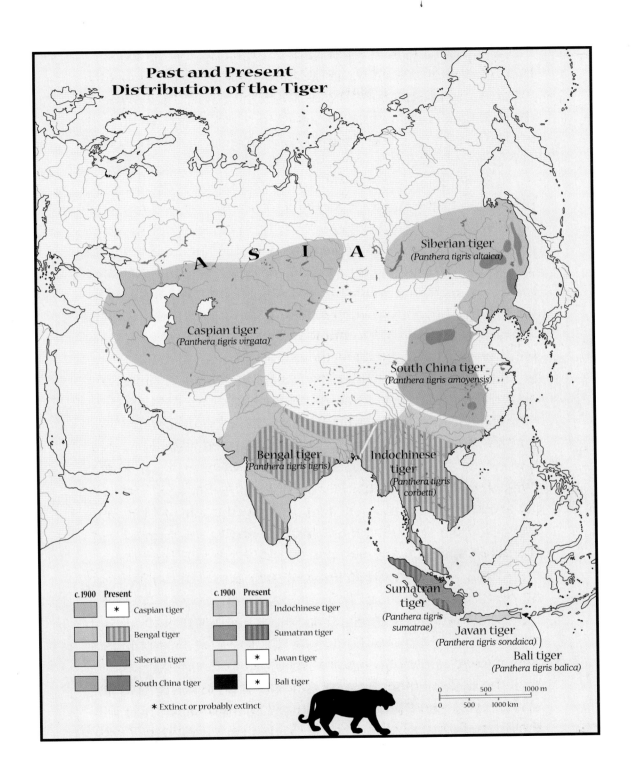

Past and Present Distribution of the Tiger

A S I A

Siberian tiger
(Panthera tigris altaica)

Caspian tiger
(Panthera tigris virgata)

South China tiger
(Panthera tigris amoyensis)

Bengal tiger
(Panthera tigris tigris)

Indochinese
tiger
*(Panthera tigris
corbetti)*

Sumatran
tiger
*(Panthera tigris
sumatrae)*

Javan tiger
(Panthera tigris sondaica)

Bali tiger
(Panthera tigris balica)

c. 1900	Present		c. 1900	Present	
	*	Caspian tiger			Indochinese tiger
		Bengal tiger			Sumatran tiger
		Siberian tiger		*	Javan tiger
		South China tiger		*	Bali tiger

✳ Extinct or probably extinct

0   500   1000 m
0   500   1000 km

the two-million-year-old ancestor of all tigers. *P. t. amoyensis* once lived throughout central and southern China, but it was nearly wiped out in the 1950s and 1960s, when the Chinese government ordered tigers eliminated as pests. The South China tiger's range is now limited to a few remote, mountainous wildlife reserves, and as few as twenty animals remain.

The Siberian tiger, *Panthera tigris altaica*, is occasionally referred to as the Amur, Manchuria, or Korean tiger. Because it is more heavily built than other tiger subspecies, the Siberian is the world's biggest cat. Specimens have weighed as much as 771 pounds (347 kg). Siberian tigers are often paler in color than other tigers, with brown stripes instead of black. During the winter, their fur becomes especially long and thick, protecting them against low temperatures. Siberian tigers live farther north than any other subspecies, in habitats where temperatures can plunge to −28 degrees Fahrenheit (−33 °C) in the winter. *P. t. altaica* used to range across central and eastern Siberia and south into Mongolia, Korea, and northern China. Today it is found in a few forested, mountainous regions of easternmost Siberia, a part of Russia that is sometimes called the Russian Far East. Researchers think that a small population of Siberian tigers also survives along the border between China and North Korea. There are more Siberian tigers in the organized breeding programs of the world's zoos than in nature.

The Bengal tiger, *Panthera tigris tigris*, can be as long as the Siberian tiger but is usually leaner. At one time Bengal tigers thrived everywhere in India, throughout the Himalayan regions along India's northern border, as far west as Pakistan and Afghanistan, and as far east as Burma (now called Myanmar) and the southwestern corner of China. They had adapted to life in a wide variety of habitats, including deserts, swamps, tropical forests, grassy plains, and mountain highlands. However, the

THE SIBERIAN TIGER'S DENSE FUR ALLOWS IT TO LIVE IN THE COLDEST AND MOST NORTHERLY PARTS OF THE TIGER'S RANGE.

BENGAL TIGERS ARE THE MOST NUMEROUS OF THE TIGER SUBSPECIES, ALTHOUGH THEY
NOW INHABIT ONLY PART OF THEIR FORMER RANGE.

Bengal tiger has become extinct in Afghanistan, Pakistan, and parts of India, and its range continues to shrink. In 2001, for example, forest department officials in the Indian state of Gujarat declared the tiger officially extinct there. Bengal tigers remain in parts of southwestern and north-central India, in Bangladesh, and in the Himalayan kingdoms of Nepal and Bhutan. There are a few in western Myanmar and perhaps a few in southern China.

The Indo-Chinese tiger, native to southern China and Southeast Asia, was identified as a distinct subspecies in 1968. Its scientific name is *Panthera tigris corbetti*, after Jim Corbett, a hunter who killed tigers and leopards in India in the early and middle twentieth century but later became alarmed by the drop in tiger populations and called for conservation measures. The Indo-Chinese tiger is smaller and darker than the Bengal subspecies, with somewhat lighter stripes. Its range once extended from southern China through Southeast Asia to the tip of the Malay Peninsula. Today, with numbers greatly reduced, it lives in eastern Myanmar, Thailand, Cambodia, Vietnam, and Malaysia. As with the Bengal tiger, a very small population is thought to remain in the forests of southern China.

The Sumatran tiger, *Panthera tigris sumatrae*, is also smaller than the Bengal. Sumatran tigers generally have less white coloring than other subspecies. Their stripes tend to be thick and black. This tiger's range formerly covered all of the large, subtropical, forested island of Sumatra, which is part of the island nation of Indonesia. Sumatra's forests have been drastically reduced in recent years, and so has the range of the wild Sumatran tiger, which hangs on in wildlife parks in the less-developed regions of the island.

South and east of Sumatra lie two other Indonesian islands, Java and Bali. At one time, each island had its own subspecies

of tiger, the Javan tiger (*Panthera tigris sondaica*) and the Bali tiger (*Panthera tigris balica*). Both subspecies were on the small side, for tigers—males weighed about 200 to 220 pounds (90 to 99 kg). They were darker in color than Sumatran tigers, with distinctive stripe characteristics. Javan tigers usually had many stripes set close together, but Bali tigers had fewer stripes. The last known wild Bali tiger was killed in 1937. A few individuals survived until the 1960s in a game reserve. No Bali tiger has been seen since 1970, and the subspecies is considered extinct. Some modern biologists have suggested that the Bali tiger was not a separate subspecies but simply a population of Javan tigers. With no Bali tigers to examine, that question will probably never be settled. There are no Javan tigers to examine, either. This subspecies was fairly common until the 1930s, but by the 1960s only a small population remained in a few game reserves. During that decade, people killed tigers that were supposed to be protected in several reserves, leaving only a dozen representatives of the subspecies, perhaps fewer. None has been sighted since 1975.

The eighth and final subspecies of tiger is also believed to be extinct. The Caspian tiger, *Panthera tigris virgata*, resembled the Bengal tiger in size, but its stripes were lighter and narrower, and the hair on its neck was shaggier, sometimes resembling a ruff or short mane. This tiger's range once extended from eastern Turkey to the dry grasslands, deserts, and mountain ranges of Central Asia and from northern Iraq, Iran, and Afghanistan to the Russian shores of the Caspian and Aral Seas. By the middle

THE REMAINING FORESTS OF THE INDONESIAN ISLAND OF SUMATRA ARE HOME TO THE SMALL POPULATIONS OF SUMATRAN TIGERS THAT STILL LIVE IN THE WILD.

of the twentieth century, however, this range had dwindled to a small area of forest and marshland on the eastern shore of the Caspian Sea. The last reliable report of a sighting was in 1958, and recent searches by wildlife scientists have failed to reveal any sign that the Caspian tiger still exists.

Relatives of the Tiger

Tigers' closest living relatives are the four other species of big cats that share the genus *Panthera*: lions (found in Eurasia and Africa), jaguars (Central and South America), leopards (Africa and southern Asia), and snow leopards (the Himalaya and Altai

THE LION IS ONE OF THE TIGER'S CLOSEST RELATIVES. SCIENTISTS THINK THAT TIGERS, LIONS, LEOPARDS, AND JAGUARS SHARED A COMMON ANCESTOR ABOUT THREE MILLION YEARS AGO. TIGERS AND LIONS HAVE MATED IN ZOOS AND PRODUCED OFFSPRING, ALTHOUGH SUCH MATINGS ARE NOT KNOWN TO HAVE TAKEN PLACE IN THE WILD.

mountain ranges in Asia). The next nearest relatives of the tiger are two other feline species that are also considered big cats: the clouded leopard (tropical forests of Southeast Asia) and the cheetah (Africa). Each belongs to a genus of its own, and each is the only species within that genus.

In addition to the seven big cats, the feline world includes thirty species of small cats. One species, *Felis silvestris*, is the ancestor of all domestic cats. The largest of the small cats, the puma (sometimes called the cougar or mountain lion), is as large as some big cats. It is grouped with the small cats because it shares their physical features, such as a shorter snout and a head that is smaller in relation to the body than the heads of the big cats. The small cats occupy a very wide variety of habitats around the world. A few species, such as the fishing cat of India, share the tiger's habitat. Kinship offers no protection if a hungry tiger happens to come upon a small cat, but if the smaller feline can leap onto tree branches where the larger tiger cannot follow, it may escape the rending claws and tearing fangs of its cousin.

3 Tiger Biology

"You will never forget your first sight of a wild tiger," someone once told Guy Mountfort, the author of *Saving the Tiger* (1981). Mountfort writes, "Having grown accustomed to lions and other spectacular wildlife in Africa I took this with a grain of salt; after all, I had seen plenty of tigers in zoos and knew what to expect. Yet when it happened I had to agree with him. I can remember every detail as though it were only yesterday." Mountfort was riding a trained elephant through a forest in a national park in India when "a magnificent tiger rose from a patch of dead grass, seized the 400-pound carcass of a young buffalo by the neck and walked away with it, without apparent effort, into a clump of bamboo. Seconds later it emerged and stood staring at us haughtily." He wrote, "Although I later saw many more wild tigers in other parts of Asia, I never forgot this first revelation."

THE TIGER'S TEETH ARE ITS MOST FORMIDABLE WEAPONS. DRIVEN BY POWERFUL NECK AND JAW MUSCLES, THEY CAN BITE THROUGH BONE.

HUNTING TIGERS SPEND MORE TIME LYING IN WAIT THAN CHASING PREY. THEIR STRIPES ALLOW THEM TO BLEND INTO THE PATTERNS OF LIGHT AND SHADOW IN TALL GRASS OR FOREST.

Mountfort saw beauty, grace, and power in the wild tiger. He also saw a superb hunter. Every feature of the tiger's body, from its teeth to its toes, is adapted to help it catch, kill, and devour prey.

The Body of the Tiger

Tigers are both strong and extremely flexible, which means that they can easily turn and twist their bodies. Strength and flexibility originate in the skeleton, the framework of bones that supports and gives shape to the animal. The tiger's spine, or backbone, runs the length of its body, from the base of the skull to the tip of the tail. It is made of many individual bones called vertebrae that are hollow in order to hold and protect the spinal cord, the bundle of nerves that is the center of the animal's nervous system, controlling movement and other body functions. The seven vertebrae in the tiger's neck are closer together than in most other mammals, giving it a neck that is fairly short in relation to its overall body size. This short neck may help the cat balance while jumping and also streamline its shape for greater speed when

Tiger Skeleton

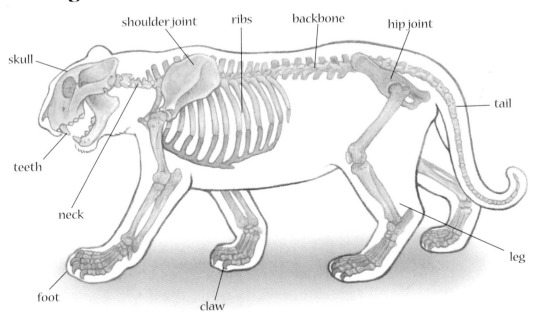

running. The larger vertebrae of the back are more widely spaced and are attached to muscles running in many directions. These features make the tiger's back highly flexible. The tail, made up of between twenty-three and twenty-six smaller vertebrae, can also move and bend.

The ribs hang down from the spine, cradling and protecting the animal's heart and lungs. The shoulder bones and hip bones are also attached to the spine, connecting it to the tiger's legs. The shoulder bones join the forelegs. Like a human's arm, a tiger's foreleg has an elbow. The elbow joint is high up on the leg— when you look at a live tiger, the elbow is the knob or point that juts rearward just below where the leg appears to join the body. The tiger's hip bones are attached to its rear legs. Its knees are the forward-pointing joints just below the flap of skin where the leg appears to join the body. The rearward-pointing joint partway up the tiger's rear leg is its ankle. The paws on which the animal walks are not its feet, just its toes. The other bones of the feet function as the lower part of the leg. The bottom surface

Tiger Claw

of the toes consists of a single thick pad with smaller pads at the toe tips. These fleshy pads act like cushions, taking the shock of landing when the animal jumps. The tiger has four toes on its hind paws and five on its forepaws. But only four of the front toes touch the ground. The fifth, called a dewclaw, is farther up the forefoot and provides extra gripping power when the animal is climbing or seizing prey.

Each toe is equipped with a nail made of protein similar to that found in human fingernails and toenails, but stronger. The tiger's nails, or claws, are curved, pointed, and sharp. Like all cats except cheetahs, tigers have retractable claws, which means that they can pull back their claws when they are not using them. Retracted claws rest at the front of the toes in coverings called sheaths until the tiger tightens a muscle that drives the claws forward and downward for action.

The tiger's skull clearly reveals the animal's predatory nature. The long, curved canine teeth at the front corners of the upper and lower jaws are killing teeth, easily able to penetrate skin and flesh. Farther back in the jaw are the carnassials, the knifelike teeth that tear chunks from the carcass of a tiger's prey. Because tigers need meat to live, broken or infected teeth can mean disaster. A tiger with dental problems may be unable to hunt large prey. Tigers with bad teeth may turn to softer, easier prey—many of the animals killed as man-eaters have turned out to have broken canine teeth or dental infections. Severe mouth problems can even prevent a tiger from eating carcasses of other animals' kills of small prey such as birds or rodents. Under such circumstances, tigers starve to death.

The jawbones of a tiger are thick and powerful, attached to strong bands of muscle—the tiger can crunch through bone in a single mighty bite. A hinge at the rear of the jaw allows the tiger to open its mouth very wide, not only to grip its prey but also to crush food as large and hard as buffalo bones. At the rear of the skull is a bony crest, an anchor for the thick, strong muscles of the animal's neck. The eye sockets are large, a sign that the tiger has big eyes and good vision. The sockets are positioned somewhat to the side of the skull, giving the tiger a field of vision that extends far around on each side as well as forward.

Like other mammals, tigers are warm-blooded and give birth to live young who are nourished by milk from the mother's body. The tiger's internal systems are similar to those of other mammals. The heart and blood vessels circulate blood through the body, the trachea, or windpipe, is the breathing tube, and the lungs are the center of the respiratory or breathing system. The tiger absorbs food through its digestive system: the gullet or throat, stomach, and intestines. Its intestines are shorter relative to its size than the intestines of a plant-eating animal because meat is

Tiger Body

Tiger Organs

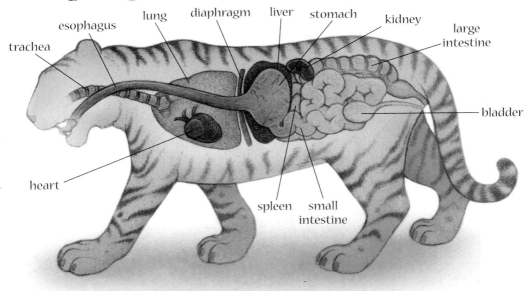

trachea · esophagus · lung · diaphragm · liver · stomach · kidney · large intestine · heart · spleen · small intestine · bladder

digested more quickly than plant material. Tigers expel both liquid and solid waste. Liquid waste, or urine, leaves the body after passing through the bladder; solid waste leaves the body through the anus at the end of the intestinal canal after digestion.

The tiger's most distinctive feature is its striped coat. The stripes are a form of camouflage that biologists call cryptic coloration ("cryptic" means hidden). The stripes break up the outline of the animal's body and mimic the patterns of sun-dappled shadow that occur in tall grass or forest. Its coloration lets the tiger lie hidden while its unsuspecting prey approaches. Although a large striped cat may be quite noticeable, even conspicuous, in a zoo enclosure, wildlife scientists often report with surprise how well tigers blend into their natural surroundings. Tom Brakefield, author of *Big Cats* (1993), writes, "I have sat within a hundred feet (30 m) of a tiger resting in a heavily dappled forest for a considerable amount of time before I spotted the 400-pound (180-kg) animal. When the tiger finally did rise and pad softly back into the cover of the forest, melting away like a wraith before my eyes, it was more like watching a ghost disappear than nearly a quarter-ton of flesh and bone."

Feline Senses

When hunting, tigers rely most heavily on their keen eyesight. Their eyes, typically a golden color, have central openings called pupils through which light passes. Tigers have adapted to hunting both by night and by day. By night, the pupils open very wide to gather as much light as possible. A membrane called the tapetum lucidum lines the back of each eye. It reflects the entering light, creating a brighter visual image of whatever the tiger is seeing. (The tapetum lucidum is what makes the eyes of cats and many other animals seem to glow when they are illuminated at night by firelight or a car's headlights.) By day, the pupils contract, or shrink in size, to protect the eye from being flooded by too much light. Unlike the pupils of most small cats, which change from circles to vertical slits when they contract, tigers' pupils contract to smaller circles. Another important feature of feline eyesight is binocular vision, created when the fields of vision of the two eyes overlap. Humans and many other animals also have binocular vision, which helps them judge distances accurately. Binocular vision is more highly developed in cats than in any other carnivores, allowing them to leap precisely onto targets as small as mice.

The leaping tiger may also use its sharp hearing to target a mouse—cats can hear sounds as faint as the rustle of a small rodent moving through the grass or along an underground tunnel. Cats' sensitive hearing also picks up the high-pitched squeaks of rodents whose communications cannot be heard by human

A TIGER'S KEENEST SENSE IS SIGHT, AND IT RELIES MAINLY ON ITS SHARP EYES WHEN HUNTING.

ears. Tigers, like all cats, can rotate their ears independently. By pointing each ear in a different direction, the tiger can hear sounds from all around it. To focus on a specific sound and locate its exact point of origin, it directs both ears at the same point, like twin fur-covered radar dishes.

Tigers hunt by sight and sound, not by smell. Cats' sense of smell is much less sharp than dogs', although it is still far keener than that of humans. Although tigers easily recognize people, food, places, and other elements of their environment by scent, they use scent chiefly to communicate with each other. They mark their territories with their own scents by urinating or rubbing against trees and rocks to deposit their personal odors from small scent glands in their chins, cheeks, lips, and toes. Tigers and other cats also have scent glands at the base of their tails.

A SIBERIAN TIGER RUBS ITS SCENT GLANDS AGAINST A TREE TO MARK IT WITH THE
ANIMAL'S DISTINCTIVE ODOR. THE SCENT WILL TELL OTHER TIGERS WHEN ANOTHER
ANIMAL HAS BEEN THERE AND HOW LONG AGO.

Liquids from these glands, sprayed out with urine or mixed with solid waste, create a strong smell that is a statement of the tiger's identity and presence.

When a tiger or other cat becomes aware of a new or interesting odor, it may drop its lower jaw, wrinkle its upper lip, and draw in air—a behavior called flehmen breathing. During flehmen, air passes over the cat's vomeronasal organ, a network of special cells in the roof of its mouth. These cells help the tiger identify chemical clues, such as those in a male's territorial markings and those of a tigress, or a female tiger, who is ready to mate. Biologists have called flehmen breathing and the use of the vomeronasal organ a sixth sense, a combination of smelling and tasting.

The tiger's organ of taste is the tongue. Like a human tongue, it has taste buds, but not the same ones that humans have. Tigers cannot taste sweet things, for example, but they are better than people at tasting impurities, such as meat that has begun to spoil or water that is contaminated or stagnant. A tiger's tongue is more than an organ of taste, however. It is covered with spiky cells called papillae, which turn the tongue into a short-bristled brush. A tiger's tongue is rough enough to tear flesh, but the tiger also uses it for the gentler purpose of grooming its fur. And if a tiger is injured, it licks the wound often. Its saliva helps to keep the injury clean.

The sense of touch helps a tiger navigate its world, especially at night or when it is important to move stealthily, as when stalking prey. Its most sensitive organs of touch are the whiskers on its upper lip. These long, stiff bristles are very movable. The tiger presses them flat against the sides of its face to get them out of the way while it is sniffing, grooming, or eating. While walking, it extends the whiskers forward or out to the side to sense barriers in its path.

Marvels of Motion

The tiger's body is better adapted for some kinds of motion than for others. When performing certain actions, such as leaping at targets, landing smoothly, carrying heavy prey, or balancing on narrow surfaces such as walls or ledges, the tiger is extremely graceful and efficient.

A tiger's hind legs are longer than its forelegs. They serve as springs to power the animal's jumps and leaps, as well as most of the forward momentum when it runs. Although tigers can spring into motion with explosive quickness, they rarely run for distances greater than about 40 yards (36 m). They are not built for long-distance running—their lungs are small in proportion to their body weight, and they cannot get enough breath to keep running for long.

A tiger is built for strength. Its shoulder and neck muscles are large and strong relative to its overall size. Once the tiger has sunk its foreclaws into even a large prey animal, it can pull the unlucky beast down with those mighty shoulders. The tiger also uses its tremendous strength to haul its prey in its jaws to a more comfortable or private place to eat. Tigers have been known to drag carcasses for considerable distances—even carcasses that outweigh them. Wildlife biologist George Schaller reported finding a deer carcass that a tiger had dragged for 1,800 feet (549 m). He also tracked a tigress had carried part of a cow carcass cross-country for 600 feet (183 m) and then up a rock pile for another

A BENGAL TIGER IN INDIA'S RANTHAMBHORE NATIONAL PARK HAS NO TROUBLE MOVING THE CARCASS OF ITS PREY, A GOOD-SIZED SAMBAR DEER.

100 feet (30 m), all without dragging it on the ground.

Scientists who have studied animal movement believe that tigers and other cats use their tails to help them balance when jumping through the air, climbing, or walking in a place that requires caution and careful foot placement. Small movements of the tail can adjust the tiger's direction and balance by shifting its weight slightly. If a tiger does fall, however, it possesses a gift that all cats share: the ability to twist itself while falling so that it lands on its cushioned feet rather than on its spine or head, which could lead to serious injury. This feline ability has given us the phrase "landing on one's feet," which means coming unharmed through a dangerous situation.

THE AVERAGE LENGTH OF A TIGER'S TAIL IS ABOUT THREE FEET (1 M). TIGERS USE THEIR TAILS FOR BALANCE, AND TO CONTROL THEIR DIRECTION WHILE LEAPING.

4 In the Wild

Although tigers have fascinated people for centuries, they were creatures of mystery until fairly recently. Little was known about the day-to-day life of tigers in the wild until 1965, when George Schaller published *The Deer and the Tiger*, a detailed account that he wrote after spending eighteen months observing wild tigers in India. Since that time, scientists have continued to study tigers, gaining new insights into how they live. The majority of research, however, has focused on Bengal tigers, the most numerous and best-protected subspecies. Much remains to be learned about the other kinds of tigers and the environments in which they live.

Powerful Predators

Large carnivores such as tigers may be "kings of the jungle," but they do not swagger boldly through their territories, devouring anything they want. For all their size and strength, tigers rely on

A SIBERIAN TIGER DEVOURS A CHICKEN AT A NORTHERN CHINESE WILDLIFE REFUGE. WHEN LARGE PREY IS NOT AVAILABLE, TIGERS EAT FOWL, RABBITS, AND EVEN SMALLER CREATURES SUCH AS LIZARDS AND FROGS.

stealth as much as on force when they hunt, and they succeed in making a kill only once in about twenty attempts. Tigers are the most powerful predators in their habitats, but other animals often outrun them and occasionally even outfight them.

Tigers' chief prey are the many species of Asian antelope and deer, from the chital deer and the larger sambar deer of India to the rabbit-sized chevrotain, or mouse deer, of Malaysia. Tigers also feed often on wild pigs and on monkeys, which are safe in the treetops but vulnerable on the ground. Large grazing animals that share the tiger's habitat, such as elephants and rhinoceroses, are too big when full grown for even the biggest cat to tackle, but tigers do sometimes attack and kill their young. Other large prey include cattle, water buffalo, and gaur (also called jungle bison). Tigers sometimes consume smaller creatures, including Indian porcupines, birds, lizards, rodents, and even crabs and fish. Tigers were once thought to eat only prey that they had killed, but research has shown that if a tiger comes upon a leopard, wild dog, or smaller tiger that has made a kill, it will drive away the predator and take over its meal. In addition, researchers have proved that tigers scavenge carrion, or dead meat. According to some reports, during the Vietnam War in Southeast Asia, tigers occasionally fed on the unburied bodies of dead soldiers.

Tigers usually locate prey simply by lying in wait in places likely to attract other animals. Good lurking spots include forest paths, river banks or water holes where animals come to drink, and the edges of clearings or grasslands where deer and antelope graze. The tigers' coloration helps them blend into the shadows of trees or long grass, and their sharp senses of sight and hearing allow them to locate prey even at a distance. Once a tiger has spotted a possible meal, it waits quietly to give the animal a chance to move closer. If this does not happen, the

RANGERS AT THE WUHAN WILD ANIMAL REFUGE IN CHINA RELEASE LIVE CALVES SO THAT TIGERS BORN IN THE REFUGE CAN LEARN TO HUNT.

tiger will begin stalking the prey, moving very slowly and with extreme care, crouching low to the ground and trying to remain hidden for as long as possible. A tiger may take up to half an hour to approach large prey in this way (with small prey, the tiger usually pounces swiftly or does not bother at all). The tiger's preferred method of seizing prey is to grab it suddenly from cover, but if the prey is in the open, the tiger will make a short, speedy dash toward it. If the animal sees the approaching tiger in time, it has a good chance of outrunning the predator—tigers rarely chase prey, preferring to wait for another chance to make a swift spring. Sometimes even a badly wounded prey animal manages to wrench itself free from the tiger's grip and escape.

Tales of tigers leaping great distances through the air onto their prey are colorful but inaccurate. Tigers normally seize their prey by rearing on their hind legs and using their jaws and powerfully muscled forelegs to bring down the animal. When attacking average-sized prey, such as deer, pigs, or goats, the tiger aims for the back of the neck. A bite there can drive the tiger's canine teeth between the vertebrae, cutting an animal's spinal cord and killing it. Larger animals, such as gaur or buffalo, are usually bitten in the throat and pulled down. If the bite goes through to the spine, the animal dies almost at once. If the teeth fail to reach the spinal cord, the tiger will try to keep its jaws locked around the throat until the prey strangles.

Once it has made its kill, the tiger often moves the carcass to a shady spot before settling down to eat it. Small prey are usually completely consumed at once—tigers need a lot of meat, and a large, hungry tiger can eat as much as 70 pounds (32 kg) of food in a few hours. If the prey is big enough to provide several meals, the tiger will hide it under dirt or brush and return to it later. In such cases the concealed prey may be discovered and eaten by vultures, dogs, or other scavengers. When they can, tigers generally kill prey the size of deer once or twice a week. After stuffing itself, a tiger sleeps a lot, often waiting several days before eating again. If large prey is scarce, a tiger can live on small animals such as birds, frogs, and rodents for a long time, but it must kill many more of these mouthfuls to satisfy its hunger.

A TIGER'S TERRITORY IS LIKELY TO INCLUDE ROCKY OUTCROPPINGS THAT SOAK UP THE SUN AND PROVIDE A WARM PLACE FOR THE ANIMAL TO REST. FULL-GROWN TIGERS ARE UNAFRAID TO BASK IN THE OPEN—NO OTHER ANIMALS WILL ATTACK THEM.

Prey animals often escape tigers. Sometimes they even turn the tables on their attackers. Male gaur, buffalo, or large deer can inflict savage wounds with their antlers if they swing their heads at the right moment during the tiger's attack. For this reason, tigers prefer to attack females and young. Boars, or male pigs, have long sharp teeth called tusks that can rip open an attacker's belly. Perhaps the most dangerous prey, however, is the porcupine. Tigers frequently feed on these slow-shuffling animals, but the only safe way to attack a porcupine is from the front. The rear half of the Indian porcupine's body is armed with long, sharp, backward-pointing quills, and the animal defends itself by backing into its attacker, who can be left with a face and paws full of quills that are almost impossible to remove. Such wounds are extremely painful and quite likely to become infected. They can prevent a tiger from walking and eating. Dead tigers have even been found with quills in their lungs.

Communication

Tigers are generally fairly quiet, but they do possess a vocabulary of sounds that they use from time to time. A deep growl is thought to be a sign of aggression—a warning or threat to scavengers who are intruding on its kill, rival tigers, or other large non-prey animals such as bears or elephants. Tigers also snarl, making a sound that is higher than the growl. Some experts think that snarling is a defensive sound, a signal that the tiger feels threatened or wants to be left alone. Like smaller cats, young tigers also make hissing and mewing sounds.

The loudest sound a tiger makes is its roar—a deep, echoing sound that carries over great distances. "Anyone who has heard this coarse, vibrant sound, especially at night, will never quite forget the feeling it produces," writes Tom Brakefield in *Big Cats*. He adds that the roar carries a "sense of the cats' lethal power, reminding us that the same sound must have produced dread and fear in our own ancestors in the dim past."

Only tigers, lions, leopards, and jaguars can roar. All cats have a set of bones called the hyoid structure beneath their tongues. In the roaring cats, a long, flexible piece of cartilage connects two of the hyoid bones. Biologists believe that this stretchy cartilage lets the roaring cats enlarge their air passages and expel a large volume of air at once. The hyoid structure may also explain why the four cats that can roar do not produce another typical feline sound, the rumbling internal noise called purring. Other species of cats, whose hyoid structures are made entirely of bone, can purr while they breathe in and out. Scientists do not fully understand how cats purr, but they believe that purring involves a vibration of the hyoid. The four species of roaring cats can make a sound similar to purring, but only when they exhale. People who have been close enough to them to experience this rare phenomenon have described it as a breathy chuffing or puffing that sounds and feels different from the true purr of other cats.

Tigers communicate in ways other than by making sounds. Their ears and tails can be very expressive. When a tiger flattens its ears to the sides of its head, it is feeling aggressive or anxious. Ears cocked forward indicate alertness or curiosity, as does a tail carried high over the back. And when a tiger lashes its tail from side to side, it is angry or hostile. Only one form of body language is more dangerous: the tense stillness of the mighty cat just before it springs upon its prey.

Tiger Behavior

"Tyger! Tyger! burning bright / In the forests of the night," wrote the English poet William Blake in 1794. "Night" was more than a convenient rhyme. Tigers were long thought to be almost entirely nocturnal, or awake and active at night. Since the 1960s, however, investigators have learned that tigers are both nocturnal and diurnal (active by day). Tigers that live in large game preserves in India, where they experience little contact with humans, are much more likely to hunt and travel by day than tigers that live in unprotected areas because they are at greater risk of being killed by humans. Some researchers believe that as human populations and pressures increased in recent centuries, tigers became more nocturnal to keep their encounters with people to a minimum. Left to themselves, tigers seem willing and able to hunt in either darkness or daylight, depending upon their appetites and the availability of prey.

Lions are the only cats that typically live and hunt in groups throughout their lives. All other cats, including tigers, are fairly solitary, although scientists who track tigers' movements with radio collars and observe their interactions are discovering that tigers are not entirely loners. Adult tigers do live apart, and each maintains its own territory, but these territories often overlap. Tigers even appear to tolerate each other's company from time to time, especially when prey is plentiful and there is little need to compete for it. Adult tigresses have been seen sharing water sources and even, occasionally, feeding on the same carcass with other females, although no such cooperation has been observed between males.

In India, a typical male tiger's territory covers between 30 and 50 square miles (80 km²). In some areas, tigers are squeezed into smaller territories, patches of open land or forest that remain between roads, towns, and farmlands. A Siberian male's territory, though, may be as large as 250 square miles (400 km²), partly because the region has a much lower human population than India and partly because prey animals are scarcer and tigers have to cover more ground to feed. However large its territory, the tiger marks its boundaries by depositing his scent and sharpening his claws on trees. Other males see these signs and generally avoid entering the territory. Female tigers mark their territorial boundaries in the same way. Their territories are smaller than those of males and often lie within them or overlap them.

The ideal territory for a tiger contains a variety of landscapes: grassland or clearings, forest cover, rocky outcroppings on which tigers can lie to soak up the sun's warmth on cool

CLAW MARKS, COMBINED WITH SCENT FROM THE GLANDS IN THE TIGER'S PAWS, WILL
IDENTIFY THIS TREE AS PART OF THE TIGER'S TERRITORY. ALTHOUGH TERRITORIES MAY
SOMETIMES OVERLAP, TIGERS TRY TO AVOID ONE ANOTHER MOST OF THE TIME.

days, and rivers or streams for fresh water. Experienced wildlife biologists know that one of the best ways to find a tiger is to watch a water source. Tigers not only drink but are frequently drawn to water for other purposes as well. Although all cats can swim when they have to, tigers are the only ones that seem to enjoy being in the water. Tigers that live in the hot climates of India and Southeast Asia may lie in shallow water for hours at a time to cool off or to get relief from flies, mosquitoes, and fleas. Even in the much colder realm of the Siberian tiger, the big cats have been seen swimming in lakes during the summertime. Tigers will unhesitatingly pursue prey into water and have been known to swim to islands several miles from the nearest shore.

TIGERS ARE EXCELLENT SWIMMERS AND APPEAR FOND OF WATER. OFTEN THEY RELAX IN A STREAM OR POND TO COOL OFF DURING THE HEAT OF DAY.

5 The Life Cycle

Wildlife biologists have spent many thousands of hours crouching in trees, enduring the bites of swarms of insects, broiling under a tropical sun, or shivering through the Siberian winter in order to observe the behavior of tigers in their natural surroundings. They try to disturb the great cats as little as possible. Their work has opened a window into the life cycle of one of the rarest and most majestic creatures on Earth.

Courtship and Mating

Adult tigers seek out each other's company for one purpose: mating. A tigress mates only when she is ready, every two to three years. Male tigers may mate much more frequently, for a male will

A SIX-WEEK-OLD BENGAL TIGER CUB PEERS AT THE WORLD FROM A SAFE HAVEN BETWEEN ITS MOTHER'S PAWS. THE CUB WILL SPEND AS LONG AS SEVERAL YEARS WITH ITS MOTHER, ENJOYING A CLOSE RELATIONSHIP AND MASTERING SURVIVAL SKILLS BEFORE IT LEAVES FOR LIFE ON ITS OWN.

try to mate with as many of the nearby females as he can.

The tigers' courtship begins when the female enters estrus, the state of readiness to mate. She communicates her condition to male tigers in two ways, one chemical and the other vocal. The tigress's body produces a chemical signal that male tigers can smell in her urine by using flehmen breathing and their vomeronasal organs. At the same time, the tigress utters a low-pitched but far-carrying moaning cry as she walks through her territory. The combination of these two signals will attract any male tiger in the area. If more than one tiger approaches the tigress, the males will fight for the right to mate with her. Although such fights can end in serious injury or even death for one of the combatants, sometimes they involve more growling, snarling, swift dashes, and bared teeth than actual fighting. One tiger dominates the situation with his aggressive behavior until the other slinks off, defeated. A young tiger may have no chance to mate until he is at least five years old because the older, more experienced tigers usually win these contests. A male that is *too* old, however, will eventually be overcome by the strength and energy of a younger, fitter opponent.

Once the dominant tiger has driven off any rivals, he and the tigress spend several days together. Their courtship includes behavior that humans might consider romantic—for example, the tigers rub their faces together and lick each other's cheeks and heads. At other moments, however, the pair bite, swat, and snarl at one another. They mate dozens or even hundreds of times, roaring loudly as they do so. Biologists believe that they mate so often in order to increase the chances that the female will become pregnant. At the end of the tigress's estrus, which can last for as long as a week, the tigers' aggressive behavior increases, and they quickly separate to resume their independent lives. If the tigress has not become pregnant, she will enter

estrus again within a few months. If she is pregnant, she will give birth in three to four months, but the male tiger will have no part in raising their offspring.

A pregnant tigress gestates her young, or carries them in her body while they develop, for between 90 and 110 days. Her appearance and behavior do not change much in the early weeks of her pregnancy. Near the end of the pregnancy, however, her belly swells. She becomes slower and less active, and she concentrates on hunting small prey that is fairly easy to catch. She also locates a den, a place where she will give birth and house her cubs during their first weeks of life. The den may be a patch of particularly thick and sheltered forest, a hollow between rocks or tree roots, or simply a dense clump of tall grass in which she and her young can lie hidden.

Young Tigers

A group of animals born to the same mother at the same time is called a litter. A tigress's litter ranges from one to five cubs, although dead female tigers have been found carrying as many as seven unborn young. The death rate for newborn cubs during their first few days of life is fairly high—it is rare for more than two or three of them to survive. Some cubs die because they are weaker or less healthy than their siblings. Cubs live on milk that they suckle from nipples on their mother's belly. If prey is scarce and the mother tiger's life has not been easy, she may be undernourished and unable to provide abundant milk. In such cases, the bigger and stronger cubs shove the smaller and weaker ones aside and consume all of the mother's milk. The cubs that go hungry eventually starve. The struggle for dominance in a harsh world begins early.

Cubs die young for many other reasons, however. They are small, weighing only three to five pounds (2.3 gm) at birth. They are completely helpless when very young, and they make high-pitched squeaking sounds whenever they lose contact with their mother. When hunger drives the tigress out of the den to hunt, the cubs' sounds of distress can attract unwelcome visitors. Hyenas, wild dogs, leopards, or other tigers—even the cubs' father—will devour young tigers if they find them unguarded. Fire is another threat. In India, where many tigers live in environments that combine grasslands and forest, people from nearby villages often set grass fires because, after such fires, new young grass

A Bengal tigress nurses her cubs. Small and helpless, newborn cubs require a great deal of care and protection.

springs up to provide rich grazing for domestic cattle. But as the fire sweeps across the landscape, it kills anything that cannot move quickly enough to escape. "Many tiger cubs are found burnt to death in or near their dens," reports Guy Mountfort in *Saving the Tiger*. If a litter is lost, the tigress will soon enter estrus and mate again.

As soon as cubs are born, their mother begins licking them all over. This cleans the cubs and stimulates their hearts, digestive systems, and nervous systems. It also covers them with her scent, which is how she knows they are hers. Like all cats, tiger cubs are born with their eyes closed. They do not open their eyes and begin to focus on their world until some time during their second week of life. The eyes of young cubs are light blue or green. They will turn golden brown as the tigers mature, unless the cubs are the white tiger mutation, in which case the eyes remain blue.

Cubs are born clumsy and barely able to stand, but their strength and coordination improve rapidly during their early weeks. For at least a month or two, they remain in the den. During this time, however, the tigress may relocate her family to a different den, especially if a cub has died or some other disturbance has taken place in the first den. She moves the cubs to the new den one at a time, carrying them by gently closing her jaws around their necks, where their skin is loose.

For cubs that have survived the dangerous first month or so of life, leaving the den brings a whole new set of dangers. The tigress does not allow the cubs to leave on their own—they follow her out of the den to explore their world. But her presence does not always protect them all. As they trot along behind her, struggling to keep up, the last cub in line may be snatched up by a daring predator. This danger grows less over time as the cubs become bigger, stronger, and more agile, but even at a year of age they are no match for large enemies such as adult male tigers. Cubs' first swimming lessons are also hazardous experiences. The young animals must learn how to swim in currents

A SIBERIAN CUB BEGINS TO EXPLORE THE WORLD BEYOND THE DEN.

and navigate obstacles such as rocks. Lakes and rivers in India hold an additional peril: crocodiles, which do not hetitate to grab a dangling paw and pull a young tiger underwater.

At first, tiger cubs eat only their mother's milk. When they are about three months old, they begin to eat small pieces of meat that their mother feeds to them from her kills. Gradually they begin eating more and more meat, but they also continue to suckle for a time. At about five or six months old they are fully weaned, which means that they no longer get milk from their mother. She continues, however, to provide all the meat they eat until they are eighteen months old or even a little older. At first she carries it back to the den and tears off tiny pieces for them to eat. Then she begins giving them whole carcasses of small prey so that they can learn how to tear the meat. When the cubs are older and more able to move about on their own, she summons them to her kills and shows them how to devour a carcass, usually starting with the soft flesh of the belly, throat, or anus. The growing cubs demand a great deal of food, and the tigress must hunt often to feed her family.

All this time, the cubs are mastering the skills that will one day make them into hunters able to stalk and kill their own food. They learn these skills chiefly through play. Activities that human observers might see as simple, high-spirited fun are actually vital parts of the tiger cubs' education. For example, cubs must learn to catch the small creatures—frogs, lizards, mice, and birds—that will be their first prey. To do so, they accurately judge how far away things are from them. They also have to learn how to coordinate their muscles to jump in the right direction, at the right time, and for the right distance when they pounce on their prey. They start learning to use their eyes and muscles as soon as they can see. Their mother teases them with the tip of her tail. They follow it with their eyes. Soon they begin swatting at it with

their forepaws, trying to catch it. Before long they are jumping at the tail tip as their mother twitches it just out of reach or walks around in the den. Their pounces are wobbly and awkward at first, and they miss the tip more often than they catch it, but their skills improve fast.

Once the cubs have begun to explore the world outside

ALTHOUGH AS CUBS GET
OLDER THEY SPEND MORE
AND MORE TIME "PLAY-
FIGHTING," PRACTICING
THE SKILLS THEY WILL
ONE DAY USE TO CAPTURE
PREY OR DEFEND THEIR
TERRITORIES. ONE CUB
WILL EMERGE AS THE
DOMINANT MEMBER OF
THE LITTER.

their den, they find a million new targets to stalk and pounce upon: leaves whisking along the ground, grasshoppers, tufts of grass blowing in the wind. In time their mother may bring small live prey to them so that they can practice catching it. Most of all, though, they learn by playing with each other. Tiger cubs spend hours rolling and leaping about with one another. They practice the moves they will later use to capture prey. For example, they may rear up to seize a sibling by the hindquarters or the throat. Biologists use the term "playfighting" to describe this behavior and the wrestling, swatting, and chasing that occupy much of the cubs' time. It is rare for a cub to hurt its sibling while playfighting, and such injuries are almost certainly accidental. The playfighting cubs do, however, perform mock versions of deadly moves such as the fatal bite on the back of the neck. Cubs also like to climb trees. They chase each other up and down trunks and stretch out on low branches for naps. (Although adult tigers can scale tree trunks, they rarely do so. They are too heavy to climb far.)

Play does more than sharpen the skills that will one day make the cubs into fearsome hunters. It also seems to strengthen the bond that exists between tiger siblings while they are young and still living with their mother. The siblings' relationship begins to change, however, when they are between twelve and fifteen months old. Their play becomes rougher, and they occasionally display anger or threatening behavior toward one another. By this time, one of the cubs—either male or female—will have emerged as the dominant member of the litter. The dominant cub eats first and gets more food than its siblings do. It displays its dominance over the others by most often taking the attacker role in playfighting. The other cubs may crouch low on the ground or roll onto their backs, exposing their stomachs. These postures show that they admit the dominant cub's superior status.

An important part of a cub's growth is learning its way around its mother's territory. The tigress leads her cubs on walks along paths she has made. She keeps them close to the den at first, gradually revealing more and more of her range. On these patrols the cubs learn which places are good for ambushing prey, how to read the scent markings of other animals and how to leave their own, and how to move quietly and secretly through forest or undergrowth. They watch their mother as she interacts with other animals and as she stalks and catches prey. Later, they begin practicing the same actions. Eventually they join their mother in hunting, although at first their headlong dashes and clumsy leaps frighten away most of their potential prey.

The bond of affection between a tiger mother and her cubs is very strong. Valmik Thapar, a conservationist who has spent many years observing wild tigers in India's Ranthambhore National Park, writes, "One of the most touching experiences in watching tigers is to see cubs greeting their mother when she returns from hunting after a prolonged absence. Her arrival provokes much purring, nuzzling, cuddling, and rubbing of flanks. I once watched three cubs welcoming their mother home and the four tigers remained completely entangled in ecstasy for half an hour." Tigresses are extremely protective of their young, and they will fight with exceptional ferocity to drive an enemy away from the cubs. But, like the relationship among siblings, the link between a mother and her offspring also changes. As the cubs approach eighteen months of age, the mother becomes less tolerant of their attempts to play with her. Occasionally she snarls at them. She also shows impatience with their constant demands for food, forcing them to begin hunting on their own.

Once they begin hunting for themselves, young tigers enter a phase of life that biologists call subadulthood. In terms of physical growth, they have almost reached their full length and height, although they will become heavier and stronger in the coming year or so. In terms of independence, they are able to wander through their mother's territory on their own and have begun catching prey, usually birds, rabbits, and baby deer. They grow increasingly independent, spending more and more time away from the family. Finally, each subadult, beginning with the dominant sibling, leaves the home territory to begin life on his or her own. The departure may occur as early as twenty months of age or as late as thirty-six months, but most young tigers strike out independently at around two years old. A subadult who lingers too long will be driven away by its mother, who is ready to enter estrus and again start another family.

Mature Tigers

A young tiger's first independent act is to find a territory. Some tigers travel great distances to locate an unoccupied territory to claim. Others manage to mark out a small territory closer to their birthplaces, perhaps next to the range of their mother or a sibling. A lucky young tiger will find a range whose owner has died or moved away—tigers do occasionally change territories or migrate to new districts. A territory's border is flexible, not fixed. A tiger adjusts his or her boundaries according to circum-stances. A territory can be smaller when game is plentiful than when it is scarce, for example, because the tiger does not need to travel far to obtain enough food. In the same way, if the pop-ulation of tigers in a region decreases, each tiger will likely expand its territory, but if the population of tigers takes an upturn, individuals may draw in their territorial borders in order to keep from trespassing on each other's hunting grounds.

Conflict over territories sometimes occurs, especially when a strong young male tiger challenges a well-established older male for control of an area. Most of the time, however, adult tigers avoid one another, although observers have seen females sharing food or sunning near each other in national parks. Some biologists think that siblings recognize each other and behave less aggressively toward their littermates than toward strange tigers, even after they have lived apart for some years.

CONFLICTS BETWEEN ADULT TIGERS MAY INVOLVE AS MUCH SNARLING AND POSTURING AS ACTUAL FIGHTING. SUCH ENCOUNTERS OFTEN END WITH THE RETREAT OF ONE OF THE ANIMALS.

Other than a possible confrontation with another tiger, an adult tiger has little to fear in its natural setting. Yet tigers do share their world with other large predators. Bears, for example, exist throughout the tiger's range, but only in Siberia, southern China, India, and the Himalayan region are the bear species large and aggressive enough to be dangerous to tigers. Bears and tigers seldom compete for the same food. Conflicts between them generally occur when a bear attacks tiger cubs or a tiger attacks bear cubs. If there is an all-out fight, either bear or tiger could win, but most encounters end with the retreat of one of the animals. Tigers also share much of their range with another big cat, the leopard. Although leopards are excellent hunters, they are smaller and weaker than tigers, which can easily over-power them. A more dangerous enemy is the dhole, a wild dog native to India. Dholes are quite small, when compared with tigers, but unlike tigers, they hunt in packs. A pack of dholes that is desperate or hungry enough to take on a tiger can kill the great cat by surrounding it, swarming over it, and attacking it from all directions at once. The pack, however, may lose many members in the fight.

The most dangerous creature in the tiger's world is the human being, the possessor of guns. Humans, however, some-times have reason to fear tigers. Tigers normally avoid people and do not hunt humans as prey, but they do kill and eat people under some circumstances. Studies of man-eating tigers in India have revealed that almost every tiger known to have preyed upon humans has been old, sick, or injured, or has had damaged teeth. Wildlife experts believe that they turned to humans as a food source when they could no longer catch faster-moving, more alert prey. In a few cases, tigers appear to have become man-eaters after eating unburied human corpses or when the supply of their normal prey has been completely eliminated by human hunting or habitat destruction. Once a tiger learns how easy humans are to kill, it will seek out other humans to prey on. For this reason, any tiger that has eaten human flesh is killed.

In an effort to prevent unnecessary killings of both people and tigers, researchers in India developed a strategy that has greatly reduced the number of tiger attacks. The researchers noticed that most attacks occurred in rural areas and involved villagers going into forests, grasslands, or fields to gather wood or perform other chores. Victims were either alone or walking last in a line of people, and the tigers almost always attacked from behind. Researchers theorized that a tiger would be less likely to attack a person who was looking at it, so they suggested that the workers wear masks of human faces, with wide-open eyes, on the *backs* of their heads. The simple tactic proved so effective that it has been adopted in many parts of India and Southeast Asia. In particular, tiger attacks on people had long been a problem in the Sunderbans, a marshy area on the border of India and Bangladesh. There the masks have almost ended the problem.

A tiger raised in captivity may live for twenty years or longer, but the maximum life span of a wild tiger is about fifteen years. The most common natural cause of death is probably starvation caused by inability to hunt. Today, however, tigers that have become old, weak, and slow are at special risk of being killed by human hunters. Some wildlife experts fear that the fate of these unfortunate animals is a sign of what may happen to all tigers. The tiger species could easily disappear from the wild, driven into extinction by human activity.

6

On the Edge of Extinction

Popular culture celebrates tigers in many ways. Countless sports teams, from Little League baseball to professional football, have adopted the fierce animal as their mascot. One of the companions of Winnie-the-Pooh, the beloved bear of children's fiction, is a tiger. Products from breakfast cereal to gasoline have used the tiger to symbolize energy. The big striped cats are among the first animals that children learn to recognize from books and toys, and they are always among the most-visited animals at zoos. In spite of all this admiration and affection, however, tigers are in serious danger. Three of the eight subspecies have become extinct in modern times, several others are on the brink of disappearing forever, and the outlook for the species as a whole is grim. After surveying the status of all varieties of big cats, wildlife photographer and writer Tom Brakefield concluded in the early 1990s that "the tiger will probably become the first of the big cats to become extinct in the wild." Prospects for the tiger have worsened since Brakefield wrote those words.

SPLENDID AND VIGOROUS, TIGERS ARE THE WORLD'S LARGEST CATS. THEIR NATURAL HABITAT IS DISAPPEARING—WILL THE TIGERS VANISH AS WELL?

The Disappearing Tiger

No one knows for certain how many tigers lived in the world at the beginning of the twentieth century. Some wildlife scientists have estimated that there were 40,000 of them in India alone, even after years of hunting by British sportsmen and Indian princes, and perhaps 100,000 throughout Asia. But a hundred years later, at the beginning of the twenty-first century, the total population of wild tigers numbers between 5,000 and 7,000 animals. What caused such a severe and shocking decline?

The greatest threat to tigers until about the 1930s was sport hunting. Thousands of tigers perished to furnish hunters with stuffed tiger heads for their walls and tigerskin rugs for their floors. Adventurers published books about their daring exploits hunting tigers. Some of these volumes were illustrated with photographs of the triumphant hunters beaming proudly next to heaps of tiger carcasses.

By the middle of the twentieth century, hunting for sport was becoming less fashionable. People around the world—including some outdoorspeople and hunters, such as Jim Corbett—were becoming aware of the decline in populations of many wild animals. Organizations such as the International Union for Conservation of Nature (IUCN) and the World Wildlife Fund (WWF) began calling for protection of the world's fast-vanishing wildlife and wilderness. Many nations passed laws designed to protect those species that scientists identified as endangered, or at greatest risk of becoming extinct. At the same time, the writings of wildlife biologists such as George Schaller were enlightening the general public about the lives of tigers and other wild animals, and nature documentaries blossomed on television. Adventurers shifted their emphasis from killing tigers to photographing them.

The end of big-game sport hunting did not mean that tigers were safe, however. A new and even more dangerous threat had appeared: habitat loss. The twentieth century brought explosive human population growth and rapid agricultural and economic development to many parts of the tiger's range in Asia. As a result, the forests and other wild habitats where tigers live shrank and shrank. An expanding human population requires room to live and food to eat. Thousands upon thousands of acres of forest have been cleared in recent decades as a result of rising demands for living space, farmland, and grazing land

HUMAN ACTIVITIES SUCH AS THE LOGGING OF TROPICAL RAIN FORESTS ARE CONSUMING LARGE TRACTS OF THE TIGER'S HABITAT EACH YEAR.

for livestock. Activities such as road-building, logging, and mining have also destroyed habitat. One especially unfortunate result of habitat destruction is that it forces tigers and humans to live closer together than either likes. Without natural prey and sufficient territory, a tiger must hunt along the edges of fields and villages, and sooner or later the loss of livestock—or villagers—will force people to kill the tiger.

Habitat loss remains a grave threat to tiger survival today. And since the 1980s, yet another threat has emerged. Tigers are being hunted again, but not for sport. Instead, they are poached, or illegally hunted, for their body parts. For thousands of years people in China have used tiger parts in "medicines" for a variety of conditions. Unlike traditional Chinese herbal preparations, many of which have been shown to have real medicinal effects, none of the so-called medicines that use tiger parts has demonstrated any genuine merit. They are based not on medical science or chemistry but on superstition. Because tigers can mate a dozen times in an hour, for example, some people have the mistaken

A SHOP IN HONG KONG SELLS POTIONS MADE FROM ILLEGAL INGREDIENTS SUCH AS THE TIGER BONES ON DISPLAY.

notion that a powder made from the dried and ground-up sexual organs of a tiger can restore youthful sexual energy to an old man. And although a tiger is strong, rubbing a person with grease containing the boiled fat and powdered bones of a tiger will not make that person strong. These ancient but unfounded beliefs remain alive today among Asian populations not just in China but in Southeast Asia, Korea, and Japan and among Asian communities in North America and Europe.

Tigers are now protected as endangered in every country in which they live, and a treaty called the Convention on International Trade in Endangered Species (CITES) makes it illegal for countries to import or export tiger parts or materials. Still, the demand for tiger-based medicines is great, and the black market or illegal trade in tiger parts can be highly profitable. Poaching and illegal trade are problems everywhere in the tiger's range, but they are especially serious in India and Russia, where the largest populations of tigers remain. Wildlife experts believe that poachers kill hundreds of tigers each year.

AT A TRADING POST ALONG CHINA'S YANGTZE RIVER IN 1999, A VENDOR OFFERED A DRIED TIGER'S PAW, AS WELL AS GENITALS. ALTHOUGH THE TRADE IN ENDANGERED SPECIES AND THEIR BODY PARTS IS ILLEGAL, IT CONTINUES IN MANY PARTS OF THE WORLD.

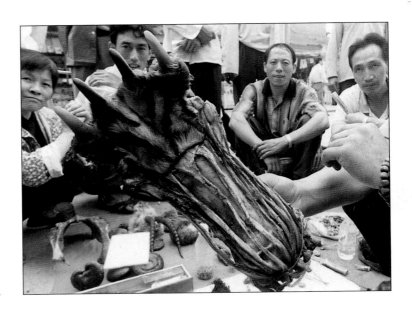

Zoos and Sanctuaries

The two safest places for tigers are sanctuaries—national parks or other areas set aside for wildlife protection—and zoos. Both zoos and sanctuaries play important roles in efforts to preserve the tiger, but there are problems with each.

Zoos fulfill two important functions. First, by providing opportunities for people to see live tigers, they educate the public and encourage interest in wildlife and conservation. Second, they offer a safe environment in which tiger populations can not only remain stable but also increase. Zoo tigers, and their parents and grandparents, were born in captivity. Since the 1980s, zookeepers have learned to use DNA tests and other scientific studies to determine how tigers are related. Most zoos now have breeding programs that involve exchanging animals with other zoos to avoid inbreeding among closely related tigers. This is necessary because prolonged inbreeding can weaken the genetic composition of the animals and allow diseases or unfavorable characteristics to emerge. Although the majority of the world's zoo tigers are Siberians, all five of the existing subspecies are represented in zoos. The zoo population of South China tigers, however, may be too small to sustain healthy populations.

In addition to inspiring people to save the species, zoo tigers could, if the species failed in the wild, someday be used as a source of tigers to be reintroduced into nature. The reason captive tigers are not now used to enlarge the wild population is that there is no place to release them.

Much of what scientists now know about wild tigers they have learned from observing them in wildlife reserves or sanctuaries, large tracts of land where human activity is kept to a minimum and tigers—as well as other kinds of animals—are protected and allowed to live natural lives. India was the first

A Siberian tiger finds sanctuary at a reserve in northern China's Heilongjiang province. Conservationists and lovers of wildlife hope that in spite of poaching and habitat loss, such sanctuaries will give the tiger space to survive.

country to establish sanctuaries for its tigers. In 1973, the IUCN and the WWF founded a program called Project Tiger in India with the cooperation of the Indian government and funds collected from around the world. The purpose of Project Tiger was to buy areas of tiger habitat and preserve them from development. It began with eight reserves and now has twenty-three. India has an additional forty or so national parks that also include tiger habitat. In 1999, a survey by the Cat Specialist Group of the IUCN reported that twelve nations had approximately 160 parks or other protected areas that contained tigers.

Although parks and sanctuaries offer the tigers' best hope of surviving in something close to a natural state, they face many problems. Some sanctuaries are extensive, but others are quite small—like islands in a sea of development, too little to sustain healthy tiger populations over time. Some national governments and conservation groups are working on plans to enlarge key reserves or link them together with "corridors" of habitat along which tigers can safely travel, but such plans depend upon the support of the people who must share the land with the animals. Many local people already resent that they were relocated from their homes when reserves were created, or that they are forbidden to cut trees and graze their livestock within the protected areas. The sad reality is that protection often means little unless reserves have enough staff and funds to maintain patrols. Poachers commonly enter protected areas to hunt wildlife, and other human activities, such as farming, constantly nibble at park boundaries. And, of course, the tigers themselves do not recognize the boundaries with which humans try to define their protected spaces. Although tigers are officially protected everywhere, it is very likely that those outside reserves will be killed.

The Future of Tigers

In 1998, which was a Year of the Tiger in the traditional Chinese calendar, the WWF announced a Year *for* the Tiger. The organization sent emergency funds to wildlife officials in Siberia and other parts of the tiger's range to combat poaching. It worked to tighten U.S. laws against the sale of products containing tiger ingredients and met with American organizations that promote

Chinese medicine to discuss phasing out tiger "medicines" and ending the illegal trade in tiger parts. Finally, it presented new plans for tiger conservation to various nations, with offers of assistance in putting those plans into practice. Other groups have also undertaken efforts to help the tiger. Among them are the Wildlife Conservation Society, headquartered at New York's Bronx Zoo, the Sierra Club, a U.S.-based environmental association that raises funds for tiger preservation, and the Nature Conservancy, which works to preserve species and habitats by buying and privately administering land around the world.

Will these efforts and the efforts of governments that are struggling to meet the basic needs of their growing human populations succeed in saving the tiger? Results from the 1999 IUCN population survey are not encouraging. The IUCN estimated then that between 3,100 and 4,500 Bengal tigers remained in the wild. The next most numerous subspecies was the Indochinese tiger, with 1,200 to 1,800 remaining. Sumatran tigers numbered between 400 and 500 and Siberians between 360 and 400. The worst case was that of the South China tiger, of which only 20 to 30 specimens were thought to remain. Unless the wild population is significantly larger than that estimate, the South China tiger will likely soon be extinct.

Tiger population estimates like those reported by the IUCN always lead to disputes in the scientific and conservation communities. Tigers are extremely hard to count—population surveys draw upon foot marks, scratched trees, and secondhand accounts as well as actual sightings. Even in well-studied tiger sanctuaries the animals can be elusive and hard to track. Some experts think that the number of tigers in the wild may actually be greater than that suggested by the IUCN survey, while others fear that the true number may be considerably smaller. Either way, tiger populations have dropped dramatically since the

A MALE INDO-CHINESE TIGER IN THE "WILDS" OF THE PHNOM TAMAO ZOO AND WILDLIFE RESCUE CENTER IN CAMBODIA. AS MORE AND MORE NATURAL HABITAT DISAPPEARS, MOST TIGERS SURVIVE ONLY IN PROTECTED AREAS SUCH AS THIS.

mid-twentieth century, and the deadly combination of poaching and habitat loss will lead to further decline.

Tigers have meant many things to the people who share their world. For thousands of years, human beings have included tigers in their artworks, myths, and tales. What stories will the people of the future tell about the dwindling tiger populations of the early twenty-first century? Will they be tales of loss and extinction, or triumphant tales of survival?

Glossary

adapt—to change or develop in ways that aid survival in an environment

ancestral—having to do with lines of descent or evolution

anthropologist—a scientist who studies the origin, beliefs, behavior, and social development of human beings

archaeologist—a scientist who studies the physical relics of past cultures

carnivore—an animal that eats meat

conservation—any action or movement aimed at saving or preserving wildlife or its habitat

evolve—to change over time; evolution is the process by which new species—types of plants and animals—develop from old ones

extinct—no longer existing; having died out

feline—belonging to the cat family; relating to cats

genetic—having to do with genes; the material within the cells of living organisms that transmit characteristics from parents to offspring

habitat—the type of environment in which an animal lives

mammal—an animal with a backbone that nourishes its young with milk from its mammary glands. Cats and humans are mammals, as are hundreds of other animals

paleontologist—a scientist who practices paleontology, the study of ancient and extinct life forms, usually by examining fossil remains

predatory—having to do with predation, or killing for food

prehistoric—before the invention of writing and the beginning of written history

pugmark—footprint of a big cat

subspecies—a distinct population or subgrouping within a species

Guide to Subspecies

Scientific name	Common name	Range
Panthera tigris altaica	Siberian or Amur tiger	China, North Korea, Russia
Panthera tigris amoyensis	South China tiger	Southern China
Panthera tigris corbetti	Indochinese tiger	China, Southeast Asia
Panthera tigris sumatrae	Sumatran tiger	Sumatra (Indonesia)
Panthera tigris tigris	Bengal or Indian tiger	Bangladesh, Bhutan, China, India, Myanmar (Burma), Nepal
*Panthera tigris balica**	Bali tiger	Bali (Indonesia)
Panthera tigris sondaica	Javan tiger	Java (Indonesia)
*Panthera tigris virgata**	Caspian tiger	Central Asia

*Became extinct during the twentieth century.

Further Research

Books for Young People

Ashby, Ruth. *Tigers*. New York: Atheneum, 1990.

Cacajob, Thomas, and Theresa Burdon. *Close to the Wild: Siberian Tigers in a Zoo*. Minneapolis, MN: Lerner, 1990.

Clutten-Brock, Juliet. *Cat*. New York: Knopf/Dorling Kindersley, 1991.

duTemple, Lesley A. *Tigers*. Minneapolis, MN: Lerner, 1996.

Harman, Amanda. *Tigers*. Tarrytown, NY: Marshall Cavendish, 1996.

Jackson, Peter. *Tigers*. Secaucus, NJ: Chartwell Books, 1990.

Klevansky, Rhonda. *Big Cats*. London: Lorenz, 1999.

Montgomery, Sy. *The Man-Eating Tigers of Sundarbans*. Boston: Houghton Mifflin, 2001.

Seidensticker, John. *Tigers*. Stillwater, MN: Voyageur Press, 1996.

Thapar, Vlamik. *Tiger*. Austin, TX: Raintree/Steck-Vaughn, 2000.

———. *Tiger: Portrait of a Predator*. New York: Facts On File, 1986.

Videos

In the Wild: Tigers with Bob Hoskins, BBC/PBS, 1995.

National Geographic's Land of the Tiger, 1985.

National Geographic's Tigers in the Snow, 1997.

Web Sites

www.tigersincrisis.com
   Part of the Endangered Earth Web site focusing on the tiger's problems and possible solutions, with information about the remaining numbers of each subspecies in the wild.

www.discovery.com/news/features/tigers.html
> Discovery Online's article "The Wild Side of Tigers," describing a visit to a tiger sanctuary in India.

www.sierraactivist.org/tigers
> The Saving Wild Tigers project, sponsored by volunteer members of the Sierra Club.

www.panda.org/species/tiger
> Tiger information and links from the World Wildlife Fund, one of the leading international conservation organizations, with an emphasis on species preservation.

www.wcs.org
> Home page of the Wildlife Conservation Society.

Bibliography

These books were especially useful to the author in researching this volume.

Barnes, Simon. *Tiger!* New York: St. Martin's Press, 1994. Companion to the BBC/PBS video *In the Wild: Tigers*. Contains color photos.

Brakefield, Tom. *Big Cats: Kingdom of Might*. Stillwater, MN: Voyageur Press, 1993. An extremely thorough and well-illustrated reference work with a general chapter on big-cat evolution, biology, and ecology, as well as a chapter on tigers.

Hornocker, Maurice. *Track of the Tiger: Legend and Lore of the Great Cat*. San Francisco: Sierra Club Books, 1997. Essays celebrating the tiger by writers, biologists, and conservationists. Color photos.

Ives, Richard. *Of Tigers and Men: Entering the Age of Extinction*. New York: Doubleday, 1996. Story of the author's travels through Asia to encounter tigers and their human friends and enemies.

Mountfort, Guy. *Saving the Tiger*. New York: Viking Press, 1981. Overview of tiger biology, range, and conservation crisis, with an account of early conservation efforts.

Schaller, George. *The Deer and the Tiger*. Chicago: University of Chicago Press, 1969. Written by one of the world's foremost wildlife biologists, this was the first detailed study of how tigers live in the wild.

Thapar, Valmik. *The Tiger's Destiny*. London: Kyle Cathie Ltd., 1992. A leading expert on tigers and advocate of tiger conservation surveys the history, life, and future of the giant cat. Many color photographs.

Thomas, Elizabeth Marshall. *The Tribe of Tiger: Cats and Their Culture*. New York: Simon & Schuster, 1994. A look at behavior in all species of felines, including tigers.

Ward, Geoffrey, with photographs by Michael Nichols. *The Year of the Tiger*. Washington, D.C.: National Geographic Society, 1998. Photographic overview of the tiger's habitat and life.

Index

About the Author

REBECCA STEFOFF has written many books on scientific and historical subjects for children and young adults. Among her books on animal life are *Horses* and *Bears* in Marshall Cavendish's AnimalWays series, as well as the eighteen volumes of the Living Things series, also published by Marshall Cavendish. Stefoff lives in Portland, Oregon.